Five Great Overtures

in Full Score

Gioacchino Rossini

DOVER PUBLICATIONS, INC.
Mineola, New York

Bibliographical Note

This Dover edition, first published in 1999, is a new compilation of five previously uncollected works originally published in authoritative early editions, n.d. Lists of contents, credits and instrumentation are newly added.

International Standard Book Number: 0-486-40858-2

Manufactured in the United States of America
Dover Publications, Inc., 31 East 2nd Street, Mineola, N.Y. 11501

Contents

1

Overture to
L'Italiana in Algeri
(The Italian Girl in Algiers, 1813)

53

Overture to
Il Turco in Italia
(The Turk in Italy, 1814)

131

Overture to
Il Barbiere di Siviglia
(The Barber of Seville, 1816)

155

Overture to
La Cenerentola
(Cinderella, 1817)

205

Overture to
Il Viaggio a Reims
(The Journey to Reims, 1825)

Overture to
L'Italiana in Algeri
(The Italian Girl in Algiers)

L'ITALIANA IN ALGERI
(The Italian Girl in Algiers)

OPERA GIOCOSO IN TWO ACTS

Libretto by Angelo Anelli after his own libretto
for Luigi Mosca's opera of the same name (1808)

Music by Gioacchino Rossini

First performance: Teatro San Benedetto, Venice
22 May 1813

INSTRUMENTATION

2 Flutes [Flauti, Fl.]
2 Oboes [Oboi, Ob.]
2 Clarinets [Clarinetti, Cl.]
2 Bassoons [Fagotti, Fg.]

2 Horns [Corni, Cor.]
2 Trumpets [Trombe, Trb.]
Trombone [Trombone, Trbn.]

Timpani [Timpani, Tp.]

Percussion
    Triangle [Triangolo, Trg.]
    Cymbals [Piatti, P.]
    Bass Drum [Gran Cassa, G.C.]

Violins I, II [Violini, Vni.]
Violas [Viole, Vle.]
Cellos [Violoncelli, Vc.]
Basses [Contrabbassi, Cb.]

Overture to *L'Italiana in Algeri*

Overture to *L'Italiana in Algeri*

16   Overture to *L'Italiana in Algeri*

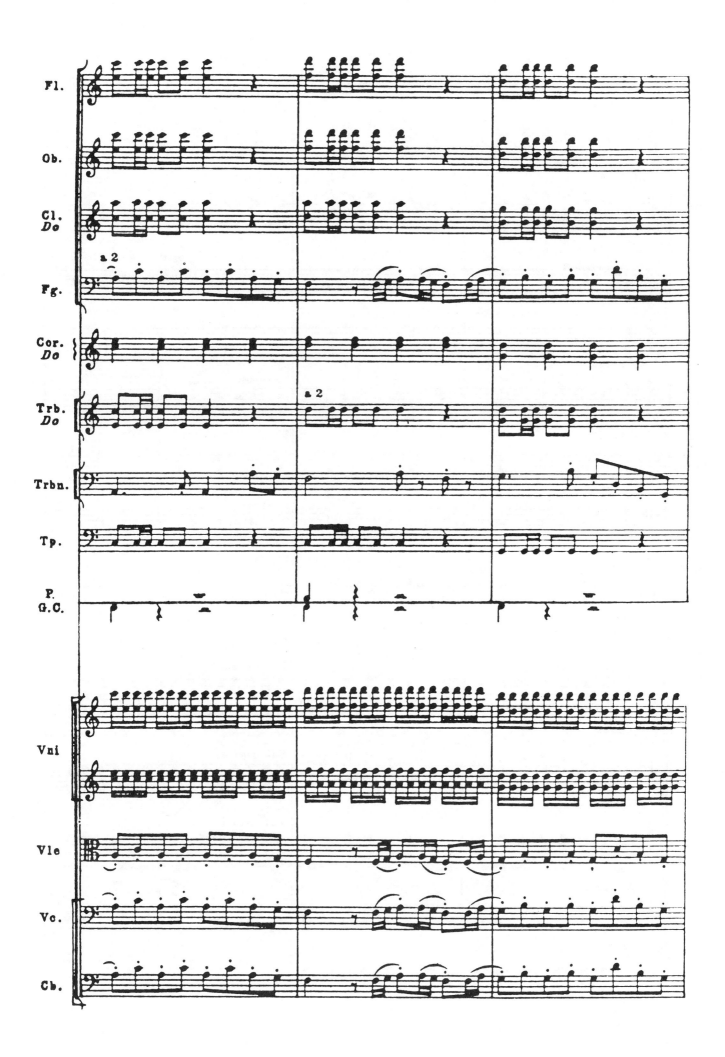

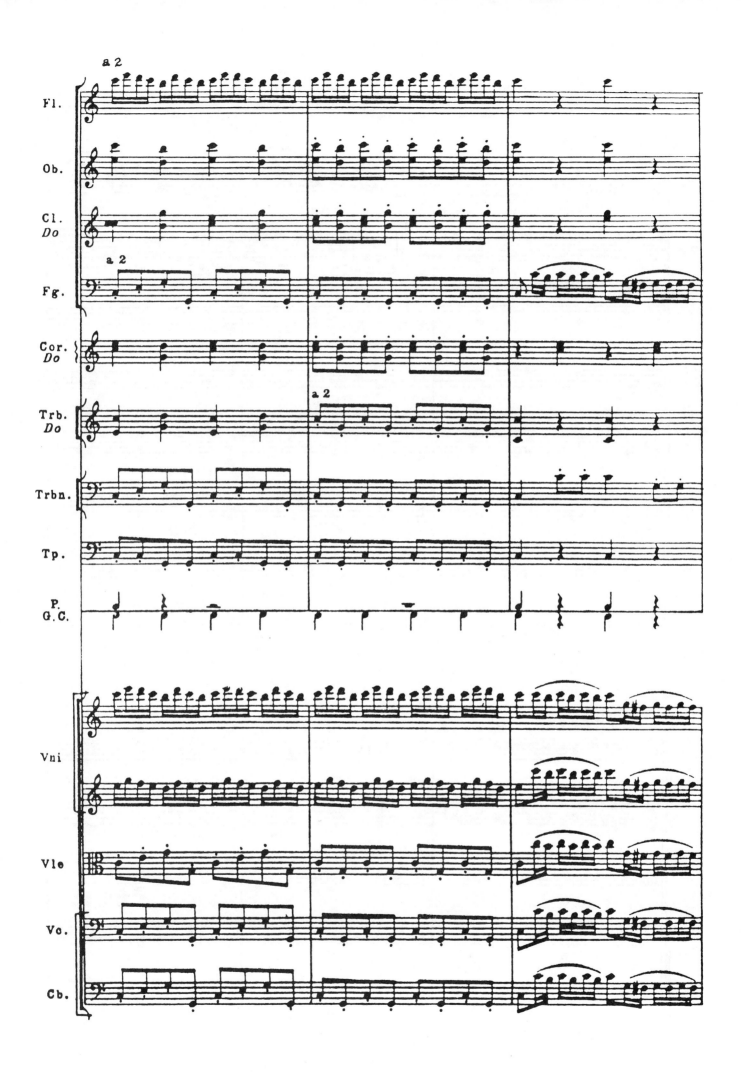

Overture to
Il Turco in Italia
(*The Turk in Italy*)

IL TURCO IN ITALIA
(The Turk in Italy)

DRAMMA BUFFO IN TWO ACTS

Libretto by Felice Romani

Music by Gioacchino Rossini

First performance: Teatro alla Scala, Milan
14 August 1814

INSTRUMENTATION

2 Flutes [Flauti, Fl.]
2 Oboes [Oboi, Ob.]
2 Clarinets [Clarinetti, Cl.]
2 Bassoons [Fagotti, Fg.]

2 Horns [Corni, Cor.]
2 Trumpets [Trombe, Tr.]
Trombone [Trombone, Trb.]

Timpani [Timpani, Timp.]
Bass Drum [Gran Cassa, G.C.]

Violins I, II [Violino, Vl.]
Violas [Viola, Vla.]
Cellos [Violoncello, Vc.]
Basses [Contrabasso, Cb.]

55

90   Overture to *Il Turco in Italia*

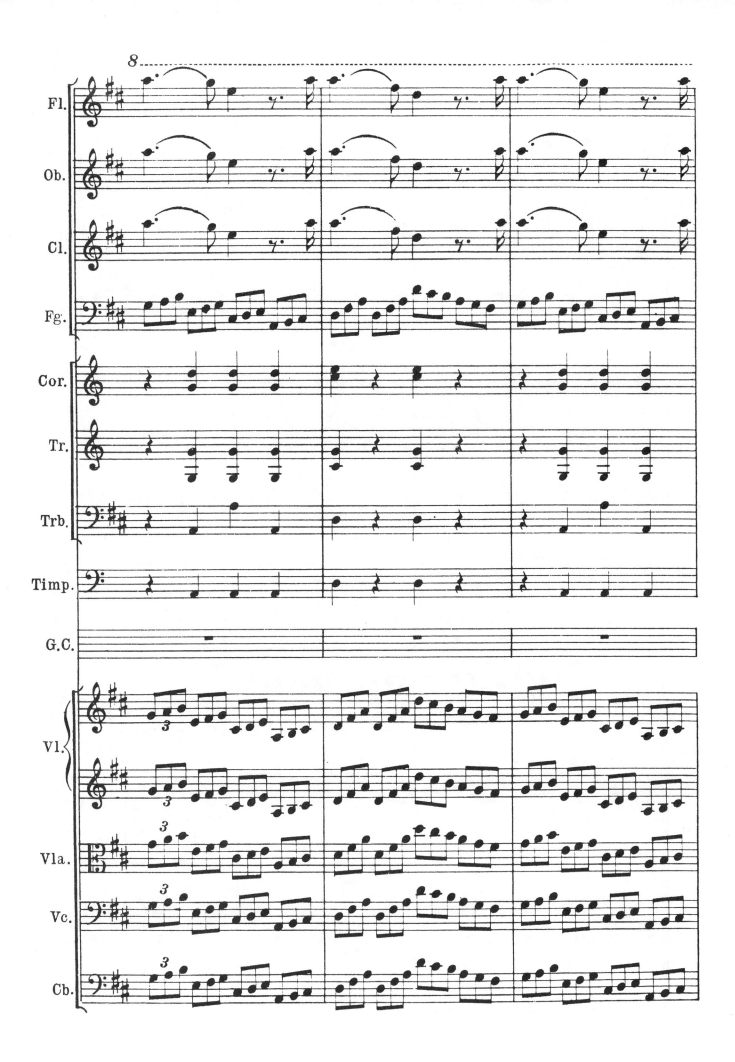

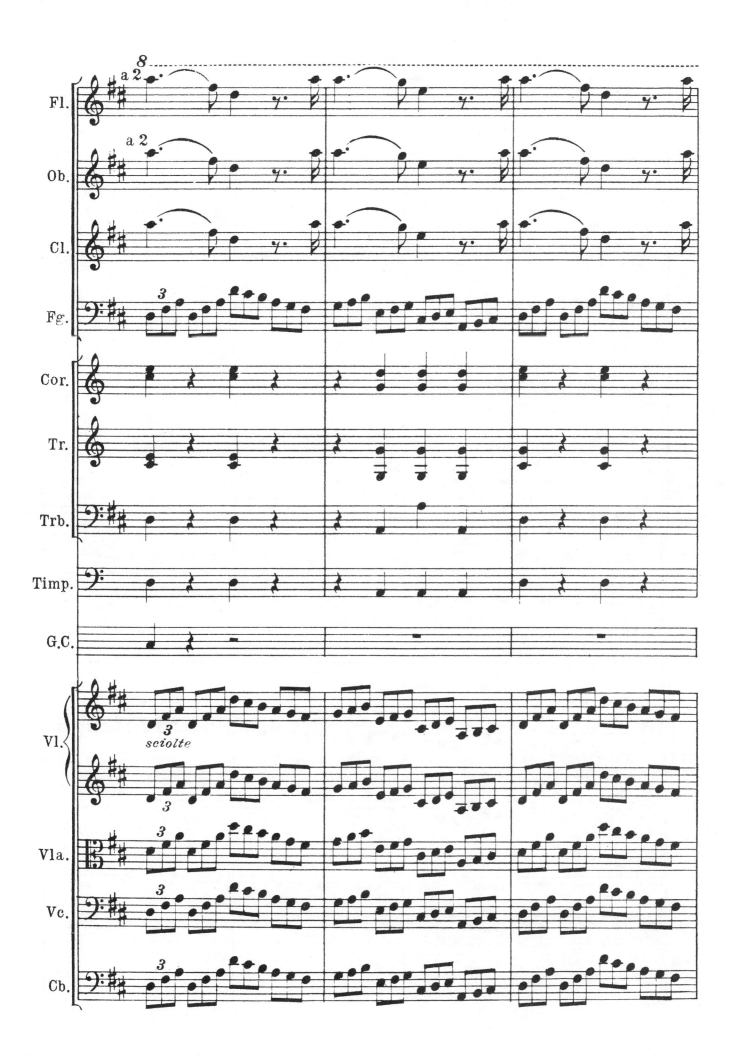

124   Overture to *Il Turco in Italia*

Overture to
Il Barbiere di Siviglia
(*The Barber of Seville*)

IL BARBIERE DI SIVIGLIA
(The Barber of Seville)

Original title: *Almaviva, ossia l'inutile precauzione*
(Almaviva, or the useless precaution)

COMMEDIA IN TWO ACTS

Libretto by Cesare Sterbini
after Pierre de Beaumarchais' play *Le barbier de Séville* (1775),
as well as G. Petrosellini's libretto for Giovanni Paisiello's opera
of 1782, also entitled *Il barbiere di Siviglia*

Music by Gioacchino Rossini*

First performance: Teatro Argentina, Rome
January or February 1816

INSTRUMENTATION

Piccolo [Flauto piccolo, Fl. picc.]
Flute [Flauto, Fl.]
2 Oboes [Oboi, Ob.]
2 Clarinets [Clarinetti, Cl.]
2 Bassoons [Fagotti, Fg.]

2 Horns [Corni, Cor.]
2 Trumpets [Trombe, Trb.]
3 Trombones [Tromboni, Trb.
    (Alto, Tenore, Basso)]

Timpani [Timpani, Timp.]
Bass Drum [Gran Tamburo, Gr. Tbr.]

Violins I, II [Violino, Vl.]
Violas [Viola, Vla.]
Cellos [Violoncello, Vlc.]
Basses [Contrabasso, Cb.]

*possibly composed first as the overture to *Aureliano in Palmira* (1813) then borrowed
for the occasion . . . "for lack of time or lack of will to compose another" *(Grove)*.

Overture to
La Cenerentola
(*Cinderella*)

LA CENERENTOLA
or *La bontà in trionfo*
(Cinderella, or Goodness triumphant)

DRAMMA GIOCOSO IN TWO ACTS

Libretto by Jacopo Ferretti, based on Charles Perrault's
Cendrillon (1697), and possibly after Charles-Guillaume Étienne's
libretto for Nicolas Isouard's opera of the same name (1810),
as well as Felice Romani's libretto for Stefano Pavesi's opera
Agatina, o La virtù premiata (Agatina, or Virtue rewarded) (1814)

Music by Gioacchino Rossini

First performance: Teatro Valle, Rome
25 January 1817

INSTRUMENTATION

2 Flutes [Flauti, Fl.]
2 Oboes [Oboi, Ob.]
2 Clarinets [Clarinetti, Cl.]
2 Bassoons [Fagotti, Fg.]

2 Horns [Corni, Cor.]
2 Trumpets [Trombe, Tr.]
Trombone [Trombone, Trb.]

Timpani [Timpani, Tp.]
Bass Drum [Gran Cassa, G.C.]

Violins I, II [Violino, Vni.]
Violas [Viola, Vle.]
Cellos [Violoncello, Vc.]
Basses [Contrabasso, Cb.]

157

Overture to *La Cenerentola*

Overture to *La Cenerentola*

Overture to
Il Viaggio a Reims
(*The Journey to Reims*)

IL VIAGGIO A REIMS
or *L'albergo del giglio d'oro*
(The voyage to Reims, or The inn of the golden lily)

DRAMMA GIOCOSO IN ONE ACT

Libretto by Luigi Balocchi
derived from Madame de Staël's novel
Corinne, ou L'Italie (1807)

Music by Gioacchino Rossini

First performance: Théâtre-Italien, Paris
19 June 1825

INSTRUMENTATION

Piccolo [Ottavino, Ott.]
Flute [Flauto, Fl.]
2 Oboes [Oboi, Ob.]
2 Clarinets [Clarinetti, Cl.]
2 Bassoons [Fagotti, Fg.]

2 Horns [Corni, Cr.]
2 Trumpets [Trombe, Trb.]
3 Trombones [Tromboni, Trbn.]

Timpani [Timpani, Tp.]

Percussion
    Bass Drum [Gran Cassa, G.C.]
    Triangle [Triangolo, Trg.]

Violins I, II [Violini, Vni.]
Violas [Viole, Vle.]
Cellos [Violoncelli, Vc.]
Basses [Contrabbassi, Cb.]

END OF EDITION